Of MIS, Oracle Database & Big Data: Performance and Scalability

By

Dr (Er) Om Prakash

Professor

SMS Lucknow

Keywords:

MIS, Oracle, Database, Performance, Scalability, BIG Data

Abstract

Oracle is still one of the most popular RDBMSs being used both by the corporate world as well as the researchers and academicians, although for entirely different objects and distinct purposes. Whilst so many other database software are available in the market, but, there are few most popular features which are simple to use, yet powerful, which makes this software highly desirable. For one, the software is scalable and its performance tuning features are such that this scalability is seamless without conspicuously degrading its performance. These features are further elaborated, explained and researched in this context. A new technique is also proposed in this research which adds a further dimension to the already acclaimed 3-tier architecture wherein the Oracle DB Server fits well. A limitation of Oracle Database is also discussed in terms of the high volume and ever increasing variety and formats of data being generated as a result of social engineering phenomena.

Contents

Introduction to Oracle

"Data is the new Oil. Data is just like crude. It's valuable, but if unrefined it cannot really be used"

--— Clive Humby, DunnHumby

Oracle, as of today, is still *numero uno* in Database Servers. (Hess, 2014). There are various features of Oracle, which makes it stand apart among the lot. This paper researches on those areas of Oracle which makes it score well and accounts for it high popularity and adoptability. The areas which the researcher thinks are best in class amongst the contemporary DB Servers are the capabilities of Oracle in the areas of performance tuning, Scheduling, Clustering and

Performance Tuning. (HP, 2009). Although there are sea of features and characteristics of Oracle, but, it will take a lot of time and pages to discuss them all. Thus, this research is limited to only the aforementioned areas which are arguably one of the best features in Oracle.

Management Information System

In the digital world the organizations maintain humongous operations by setting-up the different types of information systems. The current e-world takes the help of information systems so as to fulfill their objective in order to align with the organization goals. The companies exist in the era of digitalization and very soon they would be adopting massive automation. This can be achieved through the various capabilities of information systems. The modern organizations adopt the information system to simplify their operations. Formally, an organization is stable, formal social structure, which accepts resources as are available to them and use them or process them to provide some output. The resources available to them are in the form of Capital & labor and they use these resources to produce some output. The modern organizations also produce the output, but they have some common characteristics. They are marked by definite bureaucracies with proper division of labor and specialization. The labor can be specialized workers and all of them are organized in a definite hierarchy. Every worker reports to someone and there would be a team of workers under some authority who has a definite power limited to some role and responsibilities towards self and team. Modern organizations also hire employees as per their skills and technical qualifications (Laudon & Laudon, 2014).

Modern organization has features like definite business processes, specific organizational culture, constructive politics, typical environment & structure, objectives, hierarchies and leadership style. Every organization may have a unique mix of such features and these features are responsible to define the specific information system for its use by the organization. The features of the modern organizations and the unique impact they have on the information systems is described below (Laudon & Laudon, 2014):

a. Business process: Modern organizations gain efficiency with time as people connected with it setup optimized processes or routines, to help produce goods or services in the best possible way. These routine or standard operating procedures define rules, processes and practice to optimize the operations involved. Employees continuously learn and upgrade these routines so as to become more productive and efficient. With the help of the procedure, modern organization reduces its costs and increases efficiency. The business processes also have their effect on the information system so as to achieve overall effectiveness and efficiency.

b. Organizational Politics is a feature of modern organization as employees enjoy various positions and specialties. People have different concerns and perspective and so they develop divergent viewpoint as to how the distribution of resources, reward & punishment be effected. The difference in opinion within manager and employees define a political struggle for either sharing of some resource or provision of some reward or punishment.

c. Organizational Culture exists in a unique way that defines the way people work in a modern organization. This culture acts as bedrock and encompasses various assumptions about how, where and for whom products or services of organization should be produced. The culture promotes the unifying force restraining political conflicts and encourages understanding and agreement on common practice.

d. Organizational Environment help in identifying the necessary resources as well as supply of goods and raw material. Modern organizations depend on surrounding environment for its proper functioning. Environments also spell legislative and other requirements to be complied with by the organizations. Thus, environment and organizations enjoy a reciprocal relationship. Environments may alter more rapidly than the changes incorporated by the organizations. This is so as new technologies, product and developing people tastes and values define new environment. This has its effect on the organization, its culture, politics and employees. Some organization may not be able to adapt such changes in environment as rapidly as they may lack resources. Disruptive technologies are responsible to change the environment rapidly as these technologies substitute products that perform better than anything else. Some basic examples are like cars that replaced horse-drawn carriages or word processors that replaced typewriters (Massie & Hepworth, 1987).

e. Organizational Structure defines the structure or shape of a modern organization. There are a few kinds of organizational structures (Mintzberg, 1989). Often Information systems typically represent the type of organization structure existing in an organization.

Listed and explained below are the four technological trends that raise ethical concerns (Laudon & Laudon, 2014):

a. It is known that the computing power doubles every 18 months and that modern organizations are completely dependent on computer systems for their critical operations. This amount of increase in computing capability in just a year and a half lets an organization to make a very effective use of information systems to optimize its core production process. But, its dependence on information systems and the vulnerability to possible system errors or poor data quality also adds up to risks. At the same time, the social rule & law does not change at such a fast pace and is unable to adjust to this pace. The requisite standard on accuracy & reliability of an information system also cannot change at such a fast pace and it then the whole scenario on doubling the computing power becomes a cause of ethical concern.

b. Data storage costs rapidly declining. Companies are able to manage vast database of information on people. Furthermore, the advancement in data storage technique and reduction in storage cost lets the multiplication of data stored in databases. This triggers ethical concerns as there has been routine violation of individual privacy as lot of personal data gets stored. As the data storage techniques are advancing and the data storage cost is declining there is possibility of multiplication of databases on people like on employee, customer and other stakeholders. It is possible not to maintain a lot of personal data on these people. This raise an ethical concern there is a possibility of infringement of rights to privacy. Due to the enhancement on data storage capabilities very large database systems can be created running on terabytes of data. The storage is inexpensive and so lot of private and personal data on people is getting stored.

c. Data analysis and the related advancement have let the organization to undertake various analyses of huge quantity and variety of data coming from different people. The organizations are then able to create detail profile of individual's behavioral traits and trends. Analysis of humongous data and the related techniques and advancement in analytics provide valuable insights to the organization and help them to take decisions regarding sales and marketing and other operations. However, this also creates ethical concerns as it tends to heighten critical concerns as it can infringe the rights to privacy. The modern organizations as well as some agencies discover personal information on any individual in great detail. The data analytics tools let the organizations to integrate various pieces of information from variegated sources and these can be assembled and stored on the computer database. This can be done more easily than before as the costs of tools and storage costs are declining.

d. Networking is an example of fourth type of technological trend that raises ethical concerns. Here, the replicating of data from a location to other and access of confidential or private data from remote location is quite easy due to the advancement in this technical trend. Enhancement on network technologies like Internet lets the movement of data from one location to other possible at a very low cost. Not on this, huge amounts of data can be continuously transferred or even streamed from one location to other had a very high speed. Advancement in internet and network technologies every year let the improvement of speed and its availability to public at progressively lower rates. It is obvious that the internet speed nowadays is much higher than ever and at very low cost. Thus, there is a remarkable reduction in cost to move data from one place to other so that large pools of data can be created remotely for the purpose of data mining.

This development has further increased the scope of intrusion to the rights of privacy on a higher scale and has raised the ethical concerns tremendously.

3. Take an example of Airline reservation system / Core Banking System and criticize the characteristics of good MIS therein.

Answer: Management information systems (MIS) attempts to achieve broad information system literacy. Characteristic of a good MIS is that it should be able to deal with behavioral issue along with the technical issue related to development, usage and effect of the system as used by manager and employee in the organization. Information system has a boarder perspective than computers as they deal with organization, technology and management. These are the dimensions of the information system. MIS has a focus on management as it encompasses the managerial issues or people issues (Caldas, 2003). Specifically, a good management information system covers the four main actors, which are the suppliers of hardware / software, generally known as technologist. Then there is a business firm or the organization itself that makes some investments and seeks a return out of it. The third actor is the people and includes the managers and employees. Finally there is fourth actor which is the environment. Collectively these four actors represent the MIS. MIS has its focus on usage of information systems in business firm like a typical Bank and the environment under which it operates, which are the government agencies.

Another characteristic of good MIS is, therefore, the interaction of a bank with its environment. Thus, the bank has to operate within the framework of laws and rules as mandated by the government and the related agencies. For example, Bank must comply with the laws related to use of public investment, Bank deposits, withdrawals, and dealing with the public who open their account with a Bank (London, 2003). MIS reporting, for a core banking system, must also include the compliance reports to provide the insights as to how the Bank is operating under the outside environment. An example of a core Banking system is of Barclays Bank, which is one of the largest Banking systems in the world admitted to manipulate its reporting on the interest rates to its governing environment called LIBOR in the year 2012. The Bank was imposed a fine of around $160 million for this breach in compliance. An effective MIS implemented n the Bank could have saved the Bank from this compliance issue and related risks on operations and reputation (Laudon & Laudon, 2011).

Another characteristic of an effective MIS is that it should be a combination of computer science, management science and operations research. It must have practical orientation towards the issue and insight on behavioral perspective as well. This means that MIS needs to provide solution to the real-world problem, which includes conflict management and sharing of the resource. Typical Banking system has an MIS which works to provide solution to typical Banking issues and operations. However, it does not seem to provide a robust solution on complex issues related to behavioral management, conflict resolution and resource management. Thus, whilst it deals with the core banking operations like account management of customers, including deposits and withdraws and related reporting and other typical banking portfolio like loan disbursements and recovery, but, it is rather lacking on the dimension which pertains to people and management.

Another characteristic of a good MIS system is related to predictions. A good MIS provides managers with report on the current performance of an organization. The report is useful in monitoring and controlling business so as to provide a feature of predicting future performance. The core banking information system lacks the ability on prediction like what could be the figure of deposits on the next quarter or withdrawals in the next quarter based on some past data analytics. It is however expected that the current trends on the development of the technologies which change the current environment and introduce new technologies can trigger the current core Banking MIS systems. The enhancement of the current MIS systems in the Banks can adapt to the new technologies and add the human dimension which seems to be lacking. As it was highlighted earlier, the fast paced changes in the external environment, backed by the technological advancement trigger the changes in the existing information systems in the organizations. However, there will always be a time lag between the change in the environment and corresponding change in the organization (London, 2003).

The Characteristics of a Management Information System are providing reports with standard formats in the form of hard-copy as well as soft-copy reports. MIS also helps the users to utilize the internal data stored in the computer system for various applications. The end users can use the data to develop custom reports on the basis of the formal request from their internal customers or users (Caldas, 2003). For a typical Retail Sector in UAE, the competition is the key to survival. Retail sector is marked with many competitors dealing in the same products. MIS reporting can be used by the managers to support their decision. Effective and modern MIS reporting can help in prediction of demands for particular items for the next quarter or even next month. The advancements in analytics can help to predict the demand and supply and help the managers to take the appropriate decision. The effective reporting system to the managers helps them compare results from the past and current analysis. The effective decision making helps the organization in the UAE retail sector to stay competitive.

It is well known that the purchasing power of customer has a positive impact on the retail business. This is the reason that the retail stores in UAE are offer a range of merchandise, including ready-made apparels, home furnishing, and a range of house-ware. Decision making within senior management plays an important role so as to tailor merchandise to local tastes. Other decisions that affect the availability of merchandise depend in the liking on the color, size, brands and style of apparels and other merchandise. It is normally dependent on the on the

Sales pattern at the UAE stores. MIS provides unique application to help the management so as to implement a new strategy. They take the help of various features and application of MIS to determine as to what piece of information can be tapped from the MIS in order to make a proper decision. MIS and the related analytics & reporting can help management in merchandising decisions to support a strategy, which can also be aligned to the organization goals.

With the help of proper usage of MIS, management can also adopt an aggressive campaign to attract potential customer. For instance, based on the data, analysis, and reports on pricing and market trends, as well as suitable interface with the supply chain partners, the management can undertake and effective pricing on the popular retail products like mobile phones. The organization can provide lower prices on mobiles without affecting the organization's profitability and return on investment. With advanced capabilities and application of MIS, managers can get some information on effectively lower pricing from the system and this helps the organization to stay highly competitive in the market.

MIS also helps to analyze the data on the products which are high in demand and those products whose demand is decreasing over time. The system can have advanced features and applications to provide information on the reasons of the decline. With effective human touch and inclusion of the people dimension in the system, the suitable reports and information can be generated from the system so that the management stays focused on the products high in demand in near future. The managers can manage their inventory with the proper and timely feeds from the system and suitably stock their stores with the expected demand. Stocking the products and keeping the products that have low to very poor demand, not only occupies unnecessary space but also acts as an overhead to the organization adding it to the expenses and lowering the profitability. Hence, an effective MIS helps to increase the overall profitability and competitiveness through effective reporting enabling the management to take right and timely decision. Timing of the decision is very important in the UAE retail sector as the demands keep fluctuating and there is also seasonal bias on the products. With the proper analytics, MIS can provide timely and instantaneous information that helps the decision makers to control the stores with a strong customer focus (Laudon & Laudon, 2004).

Today almost everyone is connected with some or other social networking site and posts lots of data on it. Most of data posted by the users are confidential in nature. Though the social sites were never created to steal the identity or data of its uses, but is has been possible for some hackers to nevertheless steal such confidential data posted by the users. Originally, the social sites were created to help the users to connect amongst themselves and socialize. This seemed to be a worthwhile resource to the users and they invest a substantial time to stay connected to their friends or even family. In this process they tend to share lot of data amongst their own group or the network they have created. The challenge comes when the data is stolen and it is used leading to the breach in data security and rights to privacy. Other challenges faced by the social sites are the huge expenses they have to incur and this affects their profitability and survival.

In an interesting case study on Groupon, which was founded in the year 2008 by Andrew Mason, it is known that it rocketed into prominence in less than three years time. Very soon it started its operations in more than 40 countries, and with tremendous sales of over 70 million Groupons. on the social networking company was able to generate the revenue of around $1.6 billion. However, the sales started declining and since then the company faces difficulty in even showing profitability. The company faces biggest challenges in terms of customer acquisitions and incurs huge expenses in this activity. To stay in business the social site incurred almost $768 million in marketing in 2011 to acquire new customers (Laudon & Laudon, 2014).

The challenges faced by the social sites are tremendous and it has been pointed that their business model cannot work in on a long term basis. It is further highlighted that the revenue per customer for social sites continues to fall progressively. Sometimes the digital marketing of the social sites are ill informed and they happen to target the wrong segment. For example, these sites would send bulk emails and would reach out to people would never want to use their services. Thus, it reduces the effective customers and chances to get new customers are also low.

The revenue, proper marketing and customer retention has been the biggest challenges faced by the social sites and the solution for them would be the scale: this means that they have to target real big and quick, thereby developing their brand. Yet another challenge for them is the competition. Again, the solution to this challenge is the pace and if they act in swift manner they would reduce the chances of customers going to their competitors. Having the right number of customers and fast paced growth, social sites may still remain profitable in the long run.

Another case study talks about the privacy and security of the data as was highlighted above. The social sites collect lot of confidential data on their users and customers and the hackers tend to work on the loopholes in their security provisions. For example, Linkedin social site faced an alarming case of data breach. In June 2012, company faced data breach exposing password of millions of its users. Hackers stole 6.5 million passwords and even went on to publish them publicly at a hacking forum (Laudon & Laudon, 2014). There have been similar data breaches for almost all sites like Twitter, Facebook, WhatsApp, Instagram, WeChat, Pinterest, LinkedIn and TikTok. This is a big challenge faced by these sites and besides risk on reputation, they can also be subjected to litigation. The solution to this challenge is to educate their users or subscribers of their services to keep strong passwords. Perhaps they must provide some sessions on how to periodically change the passwords and how to keep very complex passwords. They should also plug-in the security holes in their system as the hackers are able to break the current state of security provided by them.

6. Read the case study given below and answer the questions at the end of the case.

General Electric's SCISOR analyzes financial news General Electric's Research and Development Center has developed a natural language system called SCISOR (System for Conceptual Information Summarization, Organization, and Retrieval) that performs text analysis and question-answering in a limited, predefined subject area (called a constrained domain). One application of this system deals with analyzing financial news. For example, SCISOR automatically selects and analyzes stories about corporate mergers and acquisitions from the online financial service of Dow Jones. Ii is able to process news in less than 10 seconds per story. First, it determines whether the story is about a corporate merger or acquisition. Then, it selects information such as the target, suitor, and price per share. The system allows the user to browse and ask questions such as, "What price was offered for Polaroid?" or "How much was Bruck Plastics sold for?"

The system's effectiveness was demonstrated in testing, when it proved to be 100 percent accurate in identifying all 31 mergers and acquisitions stories that were included in a universe of 731 financial news releases from the newswire service. A similar application is a

Web-based personalized news system that was developed in Singapore to track business news available in English, Chinese, and Malay, summarize it, and extract desired personalized news in any of these languages.

The benefits of analyzing financial news via a machine is that it saves on time as someone needs to be dedicated to scan through all the news available from selected source and sort this news and provided the references to the related news as desired. The machine can automatically scan the news items, perform text analysis and even facilitate an automatic -answering to the specific questions in limited, predetermined sense. The machine like SCISOR also provides other advantages like automatically selecting and analyzing news stories on the specified topics. For example, the machine was able to analyze news items on specified topics like mergers and acquisition, from the given online financial source as provided by the Dow Jones website. Machine had the ability to analyze a story in few seconds. In this way, not only it is time saving, but it also provides the benefits of customization on the analysis in terms of altering the keywords on which it should search as well as the source on which it should run its scan (Laudon & Laudon, 2014).

There are a variety of applications that can be developed using this type of system. The intelligent machine can get host of information and provide a readymade customizable information system solution. MIS would work in a given way and it needs lot of intervention by the operator and the users. The applications like SCISOR, and as the name itself suggests can potentially summarize the information from the source, organize the information and present it to their users. Thus it can act as machine based financial advisors.

The machine based financial advisors can automate lot of work actually done by the human advisors. For example, the human advisors would have to invest a lot of time in collecting the relevant information from various sources, then the human advisor has to store this collected information somewhere, analyze it and digest this information to provide some conclusion to their stakeholders. Most of the job performed by the financial advisor can be automated by a Internet news dissemination portal such as money.cnn.com provides the latest business news. The news can be very useful for a businessman but unfortunately lot of time needs to be invested in scanning the different URLs and locating the particular news items that one is looking for. This gives a right opportunity for the system like SCISOR to come into play and interact with the site to scan through this CNN site, looking only for a particular news story. The service would allow the user to specify some search terms like American airlines or Tesla or other terms to collect a particular set of news items only. For example, if a businessman is interested in getting the updates on Tesla, then this service can help. The service can also start an interactive session and would permit the user to ask questions like profitability of Tesla or latest products introduced by the Technology Giant.

As the business case study on SCISOR suggests, the reliability can be as high as 100%. In the specific case of SCISOR, it was proven through testing that it was highly effective, accurate and reliable. It provided all the relevant information on the search terms like acquisitions. Similar systems like Web-based personalized news system was even able to provide its service in multiple languages and there was a high reliability in this case (Laudon & Laudon, 2011).

Research Scenario

In Computer Science and Architecture, technologies do not work in silos. For instance, if one happens to research middle tier application server architecture, for instance, Apache server without considering the context in which it will operate may provide irrelevant overall results. Similarly, researching on a database server independent of the context where it would operate may not yield the complete and comprehensive research findings. This is so because all the components in the overall system architecture are inter-connected. One component is depending on the other and the overall performance of the system is obviously judged by its weakest link. (Oracle, 2014).Therefore, for the sake of this research certain assumptions will be made, and the research will be conducted in the context of these assumptions.

Assumptions

1. It will be assumed that advanced front end architecture, like J2EE will be used in conjunction with the Oracle Database Server.

2. The Oracle Database Server will act as a back-end tier.

3. The front-end tier is also scalable and as one is aware that Java technology is scalable, available, and manageable as the infrastructure on which it runs.

4. It is assumed that the system shall work as a three tier scalable architecture

5. Other components which are assumed in this research which shall be used along with the database server are the middle tier as Oracle Application Server, Oracle Real Application Clusters (RAC), SSL Accelerators and hardware failover and load balancers.

Due to the growth potential of the user base for the system scalability and high availability are essential. As more users come on to the system it must scale up appropriately and be available immediately, 24x7. (Oracle, 2011). The system should provide these facilities without any degradation of the performance. The Oracle database Server will be researched in this context.

Oracle RAC for Scalability and Peak Performance

One of the outstanding features is Oracle RAC. Oracle RAC stands for Oracle Real Application Clusters - previously OPS or Oracle Parallel Server in Oracle8i and beyond. Oracle RAC is the Oracle Database solution to clustered processing. What Oracle RAC does is to allow clustering of Oracle instances onto multiple machines. Each machine/instance is a node where an instance of the same database can be instantiated on each node in the RAC cluster. All instances of that same database (node) point to the same physical database files (datafiles and controlfiles), all stored in a single shared I/O structure. Redo log and archive logs are exclusive to each machine/instance/node. They would be – it's faster and changes are exclusive to each node at that point in time because redo log entries are always written first. Redo logs and archives can be shared in recovery but that's beside the point for now. (Oracle, 2009).

Essentially, Oracle RAC provides what are known as scalability and high availability. Scalability means one can serve a larger and larger user population easily, simply by adding a new node to your existing cluster of nodes. Also there is more capacity for parallel processing since there is parallel capable processing across each node in a RAC cluster. However, RAC is not necessarily an effective solution for parallel processing in the name of performance. In fact one could say there are much, much better ways to achieve parallel processing performance than Oracle RAC. It's like any complex machine really - the more parts one adds to it, then the more complexity it has in managing itself. So RAC is more for scalability, than performance.

Automatic Storage management (ASM)

Basically ASM gives raw devices plus nice little bells and whistles such as striping and mirroring - the kind of thing you get with something like Veritas. In other words, Oracle Database can now give the whole thing. It's also easier to manage because it's all in one place - and it's really easy to do. If one want reliability and affordability it, then ASM is the best amongst the similar solutions, for instance as given by Veritas. This is an outstanding feature of Oracle which makes it clearly stand apart.

Transparent Application Failover (TAF)

Another great feature provided by Oracle is TAF or Transparent Application Failover, which offers seamless High Availability Capability. The beauty of this feature is that anyone can configure this stuff. Just needs to go into the listener and config files and add failover-processing-transfer between nodes. This is nice for spreading the processing around and any kind of processing (writes) that make lots of propagation of data across nodes. This feature clearly avoids problems with too much chatter between nodes. The advantage lies in that the client side can be configured for failover and load balancing, which anyone can make, rather than the servers themselves.

RAID 5 and Oracle RAC

One has often heard this that, "Don't use RAID 5! RAID 5 is completely allergic to lots of write processing." In general, anything that may propagate too much traffic to multiple nodes might also hurt performance very badly. This includes general write processing (INSERTS, UPDATES & DELETES). However, Raid 5 works well with Oracle RAC. Oracle RAC, as pointed, is about high availability and scalability. High availability is about the other nodes continuing to trundle along whilst one of the nodes in a cluster suffers an outage. None of the other nodes will get affected. Scalability is about servicing more users (more connections), and perhaps some parallel processing capabilities between different nodes (it is sort of contradictory to the duplication of data across nodes). Scalability in Oracle is seamless and does not hurts performance, in terms of server and RAID 5 operations.

Oracle Scheduling –Best in Class

Oracle databases are widely used for their powerful tool for data storing and processing. Oracle database is used in Dashboard for storing of raw data, its periodical processing (aggregation) and storing of aggregated data. First, a collector, a special program in Python, retrieves raw data from a queue and writes them into the database in the same form. It could be information about file opening or closing, start of transfer, end of transfer and so on. There are too many of these messages to handle them effectively.

All information about scheduled jobs is in the corresponding Oracle tables. It is information about date and time of beginning and ending of procedure, about number of successful and failed runs. The access to that information could help developers to improve existing procedures. The visualization is the main problem here, because the amount of procedure logs is large and there is no use to display them. It caused a need for well-structured information. In Oracle, a web site can be developed to provide the access to this structured information. (Thakkar & Sweiger, 2009)

The web site shows two kinds of pages: general information page and detailed information about procedures. General information (Picture 1) consists of several tables devoted to particular schema. Every line of the table describes a particular procedure, it shows if the procedure is running, or finished, or is turned off (highlighted in gray color). If a procedure exceeds the 10-minutes time, it is highlighted in orange. Working time until now, start time and time when procedure is expected to be finished are displayed in red.

After the clicking on the procedure name, detailed information (Picture 2) appears: procedure run time and number of messages aggregated by procedure. This can help to understand the reasons of delays: data intensity or slowness of procedure.

In order to simplify navigation through the graph, scalable copy of it was implemented (Picture 3). User can choose the range of interest. To simplify estimation of run time, the part of graph higher than 10 minutes is highlighted in red.

Thus, the Oracle scheduled jobs monitoring makes it possible to get information on procedure run time and simplify the process of procedure development and modification. It provides lot of flexibility and allows monitoring visually through the simple GUI tools.

Tuning for Peak Performance

Tuning a database involves utilizing computing resources to process a database transaction efficiently and effectively.   The tuning process determines the amount and kind of database activity that will be generated by a given database. These activities will tend to be specific to each database type, and to a lesser extent, to each database. For example, a transaction-oriented database uses different computing resources from a database that supports data warehouse transactions. (Trancoso, 2008)

Tuning resources are broad and include the entire computing architecture; especially the network, application server and database server. CPU resources, memory, and disk devices must also be utilized efficiently. The Oracle DBMS tuning features have many 'knobs' that may be adjusted to maximize operating system resources.

The tuning process consists of collecting and analyzing performance statistics of the current database computing environment and then making any necessary changes to the database or the computing architecture. Historically, the tuning process has been a collection of manual and automated activity and has been mostly reactive in nature. Recent tuning support and products have enabled DBA's to take a more proactive approach to performance tuning.

Consider the following scenario:

An end user experiences a slow down on a database system and calls the help desk to complain about response time. The help desk calls the database administrator (DBA). The DBA gathers statistics related to the problem and analyzes them. As the DBA identifies the cause(s) of the slow down, necessary changes to the database are completed. If the issue is not database centric, the DBA involves other information technology professionals. When a database application slows down, all parts of the application architecture must be reviewed to determine the cause of the slow down. (Oracle, 2014)

Reasons for a database application slow down may be as varied as the reasons for a highway traffic jam. After the cause of a traffic jam is removed, traffic resumes normal speed. The Oracle DBMS aids the DBA in performance tuning by collecting performance statistics that are kept in views named V$_*. The V$ views contain dynamic tuning statistics and therefore are reactive in nature. When a DBA encounters a performance problem, the database onboard statistics can be analyzed, providing the DBA with only the current state of the database. While these statistics are often helpful in determining the cause of a performance problem, they do not facilitate any trend analysis of performance over time. Trend analysis of database performance may well reveal the causes of slowdowns that were not apparent from the snapshot data provided by the V$ views. And, if a database has returned to its normal processing speed when the DBA is searching for the problem, determining its cause is a challenge.

Proactive tuning tool like STATSPACK were introduced as early as with Oracle 8i. Now Oracle DBAs collect statistics from in-memory structures. This data is used to perform trend analysis, allowing the DBA to develop a capacity plan that will ensure that the Oracle databases have enough operating system resources to meet the response time requirements of the end user. Figure 1 contains an excerpt from a forty nine page STATSPACK report showing BUFFER POOL Statistics. (Oracle, 2011)

The TEST-DB has 28,028 8k buffers assigned to the data buffer cache. This is operating system memory that is being utilized by the TEST-DB and is configured using the DB_CACHE_SIZE parameter. The CACHE HIT % is the percentage of time that the data was found in memory. When a SELECT statement is processed, the DBMS will look in the buffer cache first and if the data is not found then it will retrieve the data from the table causing a physical read to occur. If the CACHE HIT % is less then ninety percent then further investigation is needed.

Determining how many buffers to allocate or increase/decrease is an important part of tuning an Oracle instance. There are Buffer Pool Advisor metrics that show the relationship of the number of the buffers in the buffer cache to the estimated physical read factor. For example, the TEST-DB currently has 28,028 buffers allocated to it, making the buffer size 224 megabytes with a read factor of one and the number of physical reads at 4,844,540 (see Figure 2). The physical reads can be reduced by over a million if the number of buffers is increased from 28,028 to 36,036. This reduction of physical reads will require an additional sixty four megabytes of operating system memory, but may be well worth the investment of system resources.

Response time is defined as the total amount of time a transaction consumes:

Response Time = Service Time + Wait Time, where

Service time is the time a transaction consumes while executing its function, and

Wait time is the time the transaction spends waiting to execute. (Oracle, 2009)

Thus, a transaction may execute very efficiently from a database perspective and still provide the end user with very slow response time. A slow response time may be due to the wait time the transaction encountered and not the actual service time of the transaction within the database.   Long wait time could be related to network traffic speed, overloaded CPU usage, or I/O disk contention.   If the transaction originates from an application server, the operating resources of the application server must also be factored into the overall tuning equation.

From Oracle 10g onwards the tuning process has become a "Performance Diagnosis" process. This process is based on the

Oracle 10g Intelligent Self-Management Infrastructure, which is part of the database kernel. The goal of the Self-Management Infrastructure is to help the database learn about its operational environment and perform dynamic adjustments to the database to create an optimal database environment. The database takes corrective action on behalf of a slow running transaction and attempts to take corrective action. Oracle responds to current computing resources being used in order to decide about the best remedy for a slow database transaction.

The key to the database being self-learning and self-managing is the Automatic Workload Repository (AWR). The Oracle database takes a snapshot every hour (out of the box default) of the current work load and statistics and stores them in AWR. AWR keeps seven days worth of data, but the DBA can modify the default settings to retain more or less data and modify the snapshot interval. (Oracle, 2014)

Tuning Packs provide information at a system level but do not provide information at the transaction/session level. Detailed session information is provided to the DBA by Active Session History (ASH). The database samples all active sessions and puts the sampling into a circular buffer called ASH buffers. Samples of ASH buffers are written to AWR. By only writing samples to AWR the overhead for ASH is minimal. The Automatic Database Diagnostic Monitor (ADDM) is built into the database kernel and uses the data collected in the AWR to perform a diagnostic check on the database to ensure that it is running in an optimal fashion. ADDM identifies potential tuning issues and provides solutions based on the statistics gathered in AWR. This means that the corrective action will be customized to the problem that was defined in the AWR statistics without the DBA having to perform the analysis function of the tuning process.

ADDM uses a classification tree that correctly identifies the root cause of the transaction slow down, rather than only reviewing database performance statistics. DBA's must still perform performance triage on database systems when a database sees a system wide slow down or a critical transaction that does not complete in a timely manner. To accomplish this type of reactive tuning all of the statistics in the AWR are integrated in Oracles Enterprise Manager (EM) and Database (DB) Control interface. EM

DB is a powerful tool for the DBA to use to drill down in the performance data. Numerous advisors (wizards) help in understanding the cause of a database transaction slowdown. (Oracle, 2009)

My Horizontal Scaling Idea

As a thorough research on the next level improvement in this area the researcher suggests a 4-tier architecture:

1. Layer for database

- Independently scalable and the easiest part (JDBC and Oracle are scalable)

2. Layer for Correlation Engine

- Researcher thinks this is also fairly simple. All it needs is a task given to it to complete and return the result, like a worker thread
- It would need locked **atomic** access to the database in the following way
  - Correlate with existing messages in database
  - If no correlation, add new "message path" entry in database

- If not given atomic access to those operations two servers in this layer may correlate the same message at different steps in their path and create duplicate entries

3. Layer for Client Interface

- This should also be fairly simple. All it has to do is grab data from the Task Distribution system in a synchronized way and create the view for the user.

4. Layer for Task Distribution (Load Balancing, "Fourth Tier")

- It needs to communicate with the other 3 layers and it needs to make sense of what data belongs together, when message path determination is done and packaging this data for the client interface.
- This layer is NOT easy to scale horizontally or vertically. The other three are simple job processing engines that don't need data from each other, while this server needs to determine which server needs what data and when.

- This is what we need to design once we have the other parts of the system figured out.

Oracle RDBMS Limitations

As the social media usage has increased, it has also caused unprecedented flow of data. Traditional Technologies like RDBMSs (Oracle & Others) may no more support extremely heavy flow of unstructured data generated through these sites. Today one finds ever grwing trend of connecting the company's data to social sites like *facebook, twitter, tumblr, Google+, Whatsapp, skype*, etc and the data may come in any format and is classified as unstructured data. (Carter & Levy, 2012). There are several formats of data like voice & image data, and these serve various company needs for some processing or serve as a process.

Traditional ways of RDBMS, SQL or other others need the data in structured or given format. Moreover, irrespective of performance tuning and other features, there seems to be an upper limit, beyond which the traditional technologies may beak-down. The new technologies known as Big Data Technologies are currently being researched, developed and refined to handle such high loads. "BIG

DATA" itself refers to very high loads and collection of unstructured datasets. (Bigdataq.com, 2014)

Big Data Technologies appear to be the signs of future as they come into play whenever there is:

- Very High Volume of data generated

- Very High Velocity in data flows

- Very High Variety coming p in different and unstructured data formats.

Bibliography

Amazon. (n.d.). *Getting Started with Amazon EC2 Windows Instances.* Amazon.com. Retrieved from http://docs.aws.amazon.com/AWSEC2/latest/WindowsGuide/EC2 Win_GetStarted.html

Bigdataq.com. (2014). *Big Data analytics.* Bigdataq.com.

Carter, B., & Levy, J. (2012). *Facebook Marketing: Leveraging Facebook's Features for your marketing campaigns. .* Pearson Education.

Chandani, A., & Neerja, B. (2007). *Knowledge management: an overview & its impact on software .* IEEEXPlore.

Data&Society Research Institue. (2014). *The Social, Cultural & Ethical Dimensions of "Big Data".* Data&Society. Retrieved from

http://www.datasociety.net/pubs/2014-0317/AlgorithmicAccount
abilityNotes.pdf

DatabaseSkill. (2011). *CGI ASP PHP JSP ASP.net Comparison.*
http://www.databaseskill.com/2211663/.

Dela Torre, K. (2013). *Oracle Cloud Central.* Oracle.com.

Hess, K. (2014). *Top 10 Enterprise Database Systems to Consider.*
ITBusinessEdge.

Hughes, T. (1987). *The evolution of large technological systems.* MIT Press,
Cambridge MA, London, pp. 51–82.

Oracle. (2009). *The Benefits of Risk Assessment for Projects, Portfolios,
and Businesses .* Oracle White Paper.

PMP. (2014). *Introducing Project Risk Management.*
http://www.euroi.ktu.lt/lt/images/stories/Paskaitos/ch11.pdf.

Rousseau, D. (2006). *Is there such a thing as "evidence-based
management?* Academy of Management Review, Vol. 31, No. 2,
pp. 256–69.

SAP. (2013). *SAP Cloud Applications Studio – A powerful business tool for
freedom, flexibility, and speed in the Cloud.* SAP.com.

*SAP Cloud Applications Studio – A powerful business tool for freedom,
flexibility, and speed in the Cloud.* SAP.

Tranfield, . D., & Denyer, D. (2004). *'Linking theory to practice: a grand
challenge for management research in the 21st century?'.*
Organization Management Journal, Vol. 1, No. 1, pp. 10–14.

Caldas, M. P. (2003). Management information systems: managing
the digital firm. Revista de Administração Contemporânea,
7(1), 223-223.

Laudon, K. C. & Laudon, J.P. (2014). Management information systems: Managing the digital firm. Pearson Education India.

Laudon, K. C., & Laudon, J. P. (2011). Essentials of management information systems. Upper Saddle River: Pearson.

Laudon, K. C., & Laudon, J. P. (2004). Managing the digital firm. Managing Information Systems, 197-200.

London, K. C. (2003). Essentials of management information systems: managing the digital firm (No. 04; T58. 6, L3 2003.).

Massie, J. L., & Hepworth, K. (1987). Essentials of management. Englewood Cliffs, NJ: Prentice-Hall.

Mintzberg, H. (1989). Mintzberg on management: Inside our strange world of organizations. Simon and Schuster.